Contents

About the Author

Ian Baxter is a military historian who specialises in German twentieth-century military history. He has written more than seventy books, including *Poland: The Eighteen-Day Victory March*; *Panzers in North Africa*; *The Waffen-SS Ardennes Offensive*; *The Western Campaign*; *The 12th SS Panzer Division Hitlerjugend*; *Waffen-SS on the Western Front*; *Waffen-SS on the Eastern Front*; *The Red Army at Stalingrad*; *Elite German Forces of World War II*; *Armoured Warfare: German Tanks of World War II*; *Blitzkrieg*; *Panzer Divisions at War*; *German Armoured Vehicles of World War Two*; *Last Two Years of the Waffen-SS at War*; *German Soldier Uniforms and Insignia*; *German Guns of the Third Reich*; *From Retreat to Defeat: The Last Years of the German Army at War 1943–45* and, most recently, *The Sixth Army and the Road to Stalingrad*.

He has written over a hundred articles, including 'Last days of Hitler', 'Wolf's Lair', 'The Story of the V1 and V2 Rocket Programme', 'Secret Aircraft of World War Two', 'Rommel at Tobruk', 'Hitler's War with his Generals', 'Secret British Plans to Assassinate Hitler', 'The SS at Arnhem', 'Hitlerjugend', 'Battle of Caen 1944', 'Gebirgsjäger at War', 'Panzer Crews', 'Hitlerjugend Guerrillas', 'Last Battles in the East', 'The Battle of Berlin' and many more.

He has also reviewed numerous military studies for publication, supplied thousands of photographs and important documents to various publishers and film production companies worldwide, and he lectures to schools, colleges and universities throughout the United Kingdom and the Republic of Ireland.

IMAGES OF WAR

TANKS & ARMOUR IN UKRAINE 1941–44

RARE PHOTOGRAPHS FROM WARTIME ARCHIVES

Ian Baxter

Pen & Sword
MILITARY

First published in Great Britain in 2025 by
PEN & SWORD MILITARY
an imprint of Pen & Sword Books Ltd
Yorkshire – Philadelphia

ISBN 978-1-03612-255-3

A CIP catalogue record for this book is available from the British Library.

Typeset by Concept, Huddersfield, West Yorkshire, HD4 5JL.
Printed and bound in England by CPI Group (UK) Ltd, Croydon, CR0 4YY.

The Publisher's authorised representative in the EU for product safety is Authorised Rep Compliance Ltd, Ground Floor, 71 Lower Baggot Street, Dublin D02 P593, Ireland – www.arccompliance.com

For a complete list of Pen & Sword titles please contact
PEN & SWORD BOOKS LTD
47 Church Street, Barnsley, South Yorkshire, S70 2AS, England
E-mail: enquiries@pen-and-sword.co.uk
Website: www.pen-and-sword.co.uk
or
PEN & SWORD BOOKS
1950 Lawrence Road, Havertown, PA 19083, USA
E-mail: uspen-and-sword@casematepublishers.com
Website: www.penandswordbooks.com

Introduction

When the German war machine launched its attack against the Soviet Union on 22 June 1941, Adolf Hitler had given priority first to the capture of Ukraine, which was against the advice of his generals. In order to secure Ukraine quickly and effectively, the German Army Group South entrusted its powerful Panzer Group 1 to lead the spearhead through the country. It included the III, XIV and XLVIII Army Corps (motorized) with five Panzer divisions and four motorized divisions (two of them SS) equipped with 799 tanks. Unlike their enemy, German armoured units had effective command, control, communication, and a massive supply of ammunition and support formations coupled with considerable combat experience and extensive training. What followed in the heartlands of Ukraine was a series of powerful wide sweeping deep penetrating armoured attacks toward the Dnieper River. Places like Dubno, Brody, Kyiv, Crimea, and Kharkov saw heavy armoured fighting.

This book in the Image of War series is a highly-illustrated record of German tanks and armour that fought in Ukraine between 1941 and 1944. It describes how these deadly machines fought and supported and infantry on the battlefield. It depicts how these formidable weapons were adapted and up-gunned to face the ever-increasing enemy threat. With rare and often published photographs this book provides a unique insight into German armour in Ukraine from its early triumphant days in 1941 and 1942 to its slow and painful retreat in 1944.

Chapter One

Invasion of Ukraine 1941

When the German invasion of Russia was launched on 22 June 1941, Code-named 'Operation Barbarossa', the German war machine divided its forces into three Army Groups; North, under Field-Marshal Ritter von Leeb; Centre, under Field-Marshal Fedor von Bock; and in the South, under Field-Marshal Gerd von Rundstedt. They had three objectives: Leningrad, Moscow and Ukraine.

In the south, Rundstedt boasted the 6th Army, 7th Army, 11th, Romanian 4th Army, Romanian Army Group Antonescu, and Panzergruppe 1, along with a mix of Hungarian, Italian and Slovak units. The main thrust on the southern front was directed between the southern edge of the Pripet Marshes and the foothills of the Carpathian Mountains with the main objective of capturing Ukraine.

In order to secure Ukraine quickly and effectively, Panzer Group 1 was to lead the spearhead through the country. It included the III, XIV and XLVIII Army Corps (motorized) with five Panzer divisions and four motorized divisions (two of them SS) equipped with 799 tanks. Panzer Group 1 was commanded by General von Kleist and his objective was to spearhead his powerful armoured columns, secure the Bug River and drive to Kyiv.

The first few hours of the drive went well, but Russian intelligence had received reports of Kleist's armoured attack, and its intention. On the Southwest Front, under the command of General Mikhail Kirponos, he ordered six Soviet mechanized corps, with some 2,500 tanks, to be moved and concentrated along the flanks of Panzer Group 1. Although initially the order was considered purely a defensive action, they realized that the Panzer formations would be caught by surprise, so a planned attempt for a pincer movement from the north was made utilizing the Soviet 5th Army and south 6th Army. They would both meet west of Dubno where they could possibly trap units of the 6th and 17th German Armies on the northern flank of Army Group South. Forward units predicting the path of the Panzers then began laying mines and placed anti-tank guns in surrounding forests and undergrowth to slow down the German advance, so it would be easier to knock out enemy armour. Because much of the German armour comprised of light Pz.Kpfz.I and II tanks, they were deemed easy prey for Russian anti-tank gunners.

During the early hours of 24 June, the 1 Panzer Army Group launched its attack. However, by this time the 11th and 16th Panzer Divisions had already penetrated some 40 miles into Russian territory and were preparing to move out into the Soviet heartlands. The 13th and 14th Panzer Divisions were already on the road towards Lutsk with the objective of taking the Styr River. Yet unbeknown to the Panzer units there were three potent Soviet formations ready to attack comprising of some 1948 tanks distributed between 4th, 8th, and 15th Mechanized Corps alone. Other mechanized formations in the area consisted of the 9th, 19th and 22nd Mechanized Corps, which boasted some 1481 tanks. However, in spite of these impressive numbers of armour, many of the Russian tank crews were ill-prepared, lacked training, lacked fuel, ammunition, and spare parts which assured that actual operational vehicles were dramatically fewer in numbers to confront the Germans in the field.

Confronting the Soviet arsenal, the German 9th, 11th, 13th,14th and 16th Panzer Divisions comprised of some 728 tanks. Unlike their enemy, their units had effective command, control, communication, and a massive supply of ammunition and support units coupled with considerable combat experience and extensive training. But whatever lack of training, support and combat effectiveness the Soviets had, they were determined to throw six mechanized corps under the command of 5th Army to the north and the 6th Army to the south, under the general direction of Southwestern Front commander Kirponos.

The main part of the attack would be unleashed near the town of Brody in western Ukraine. The Soviet counter-attack surprised the advanced Panzer echelons that were advancing at speed through the countryside bound for Kyiv. Initially, the Russian attack was piecemeal, as the bulk of its forces were not able to be brought into position until two days later. The 4th, 8th, 9th, and 19th Mechanized Corps were still on the march and supporting infantry corps. Yet, despite the lack of support, the Russians launched their assault attacking advancing German troops and armour with T-34s and KV-1s. What followed was the battle of Brody with Red Army infantry and tanks bitterly contesting every part of ground in the field. It soon became a fierce contest of attrition, and although the Russians showed great fortitude and determination, they were constantly hampered by lack of weapons and manpower needed to sustain them on the battlefield.

On 25 June, the Soviet 10th Tank Division attacked the 11th Panzer Division knocking out twenty Panzers and losing six T-34 tanks and twenty BT tanks. The next day it reported that it disabled twenty-three German tanks and an infantry battalion near Radekhiv, losing thirteen KV and twelve BT-7 tanks. However, the situation for the Soviet tank crews looked grim. The ferocity of the German attack was immense and without respite. Coupled with the lack of support and ammunition, Red Army units reluctantly withdrew after nearly 48 hours of almost continuous battle.

Yet, in spite the heavy losses. the Russians continued to contest the panzer units in the area. Near Dubno, fighting was also very fierce and within a couple of days of heavy action against Pz.Kpfw.IIs, the 19th Mechanized Division had lost thirty-two tanks trying to reach the town. The 8th Mechanized Corps, however, fared much better during its initial attack in the direction of Brody-Berestechko against parts of the 11th Panzer Division. In some areas of the front, Russian tank men managed to achieve some success, smashing through hastily prepared German anti-tank gun crews and their supporting tanks from the 48th Panzer Corps.

Though the Russians had stemmed the panzer group drive around Brody, there were still too few in numbers to change the situation and many Red Army crews were fighting chaotically with no cohesion. As a result, remnants of the Russian mechanized units reluctantly begun to withdrew eastwards before it was destroyed. The Battle of Brody between Panzer Group 1 and the Soviet Mechanized Corps was the fiercest tank battle of the whole invasion, lasting four full days. Yet, in spite the German victory, the Panzer crews had taken a severe battering, but it survived the battle and was still capable of continuing operations eastwards. It is unclear how many German tanks were destroyed in the battle, but the force did lose 100 of its Panzers during the first two weeks of the war. For the Soviets, this particular engagement was a tactical defeat and its attack saw a huge number of tanks, between 800 and 1,000, lost as a result.

Elsewhere across western Ukraine, Germans Panzer and armoured forces made astonishing progress towards the Dnieper River even though they were continually harassed by strong Russian forces coupled with the Soviet military's scorched-earth policy. Again and again, the Russians were overwhelmed by the rapid German onslaught. By August 1941, the 6th Army had swung out east of Kyiv as German forces began mopping up the last remnants in and around the besieged city. The battle for Kyiv was launched on 16 September by the German XXIX Army Corps of the 6th Army. The 71st and 296th infantry divisions led the attack, smashing through Red Army defensive positions. Supporting the attack were the 95th Infantry Division and the 3rd Battalion of the 77th Sturmgeschütz Regiment.

When the battle of Kyiv finally ended on 21 September, almost 665,000 Russian troops had been captured in the encirclement. The loss of Kyiv and the destruction of the Russian Southwestern Front were considered an unparalleled defeat of the Red Army. Exhilarated by the fall of Kyiv, German forces mercilessly pushed forward, leaving a trail of devastation in its wake. The whole Russian forces were now in chaotic state and could no longer maintain any cohesion in both in defence and attack. As a result, across the whole of Reichenau's front tanks and supporting infantry hammered deeper, and the guns of the infantry divisions lengthened their range. The bulk of Army Group South was continuing its effort to drive east and southeast to secure the Donetz river line and Rostov before winter set in. Extensive plans were also made by General Manstein to assault the Crimea peninsula with his 11th Army which he took over in September 1941.

For the attack into the Crimea, he had been assigned two divergent missions: to overrun the Crimea and to take Rostov. On 24 September 1941, Manstein attacked south into the Perekop with General Erik Hansen's LIV Corps, with General Kuebler's XLIX Gebirgsjager-Corps in reserve. They had been given specific orders to exploit any breakthrough and drive to Sevastopol and advance southwards, with its leading armoured units to the great Soviet naval fortress on the southwestern tip of the peninsula. Manstein was to drive through the Crimea to Sevastopol but all he had to defend his eastern flank was General Hans von Salmuth's 30th Corps and six unreliable Romanian brigades.

On 28 September Hansen's LIV Corps attacked towards Perekop against six Soviet divisions and fought a bitter action there. Although Hansen's Corps incurred heavy casualties, it managed to capture 10,000 prisoners, 112 tanks, and 135 guns in the process. But the victory could not be exploited, because the Soviets attacked Manstein's eastern flank. Whilst 30th Corps held its ground under merciless enemy fire, the Romanians collapsed, and Manstein had to rush Kuebler's Corps to the Nogav Steppe. It seemed that the Red Army had temporarily halted the German drive through the Crimea, but it had exposed its right flank to an attack by Kleist's 1st Panzer-Army to the north. From 5–10 October both Kleist and Manstein cooperated in a battle of encirclement on the Sea of Azov. In the process, they managed to destroy the Red Army's 18th Army. The Germans, however, once again incurred heavy casualties and gave the Russians three weeks to reinforce Sevastopol and the Crimea.

At the end of October, the Germans launched an attack against the heavily fortified port of Sevastopol. The German attack went well and units captured the Balaklava Hills, and then drove armoured units supported by troops into the city of Sevastopol from the north, north-east and east, but were beaten back. The Germans then encircled the city. During this time, the city was reinforced by the sea, receiving the bulk of Russian troops evacuated from Odessa.

Through December 1941, Manstein's forces pounded the port with heavy artillery and on 17 December, six German infantry divisions and two Romanian brigades with 1,275 guns and mortars, over 150 tanks and 300 aircraft launched a second attack. Although German formations had managed to get within a mile of Severnaia Bay, they were beaten back by strong Soviet resistance.

For the next two weeks, the Germans dug-in to positions surrounding the bay and Sevastopol and continued a series of probing attacks and heavy, unrelenting artillery bombardments. Yet despite the resilience of their enemy, Manstein knew that the Russians would not be able to hold their positions indefinitely.

Elsewhere in Ukraine, territorial gains were more successful. In spite of the rapid advance through Ukraine, much of the army units were not mechanized. In the 6th and 7th Army alone, there were some 25,000 horses that were used to move guns and supplies. Although this type of transportation did not cause its commanders initial concern, by the time the army arrived at the higher Donets River in October, the weather began to change. Cold driving rain fell on the Army Groups front and within hours the Russian countryside had been turned into a quagmire with roads and fields becoming virtually impassable. Many of the roads leading west from Kyiv, towards Poltava and Kharkov had become boggy swamps.

Although tanks and other tracked vehicles managed to push through the mire at slow pace, animal draft, trucks and other wheeled vehicles became hopelessly stuck in deep boggy mud. To make matters worse, during November, the German supply lines through Ukraine became increasingly overstretched, their vehicles were breaking down, and casualty returns were mounting. Supply lines via rail from Lwow into the central part of the country towards Cherkasy were also delayed by bad weather and stiff resistance. As the situation deteriorated further in northeastern Ukraine, Rundstedt, against Hitler's orders, ordered Kleist's 1st Panzer Army to evacuate Rostov and fall back over the Mius River, some 60 miles west of the city. On the night of 30 November, Rundstedt was relieved of his command and replaced by Reichenau. As a commander, Reichenau was a truly proficient fastidious general, but he lacked decisiveness and regarded the *Führer* as a flawless military expert.

A column of Sturmgeschütz.III assault guns advance through a field during the opening phase of the invasion of Russia. During Barbarossa, the StuG.III was detailed to the infantry divisions that fought at focal points in the battle. Although the StuG.III was an effective infantry support weapon because it had a fixed turret, it was not well suited to urbanized combat and was therefore only used in a limited role during close quarter engagements trying to capture towns and cities.

(**Above**) For the invasion of the Soviet Union, the Panzerwaffe boast 439 Pz.Kpfw.IVs. Here, in this photograph, a Pz.Kpfw.IV Ausf.C advances along a road into Ukraine. Around forty were produced before it was replaced with the newly-improved Ausf.D variant.

(**Opposite, above**) A Pz.Kpfw.III Ausf.J advances across a field supported by infantry. For Barbarossa, the Panzerwaffe totalled 965 Pz.Kpfw. IIIs for the invasion. This was, by far, the largest contingent of armour to fight in the war. For the first four months of the war in Ukraine, the Pz.Kpfw.III with its 5cm L/42 gun proved its worth on the battlefield, but together with the vast expanse of terrain and being too few dispersed along an ever-increasing front, constant breakdowns became common.

(**Opposite, below**) Two Sturmgeschütz.III Ausf.B are followed by an Sd.Kfz.252 ammunition supply half-track, with additional ammunition in the small trailer during the opening phase of Operation Barbarossa. During the first weeks of the invasion of Ukraine, the StuG.III performed very well in an infantry support role. The StuG had a crew of four and came equipped with a 7.5cm StuK 37 L/24 gun capable of traversing from 12.5 degrees left to 12.5 degrees right.

An Sd.Kfz.223 Leichter Panzerspähwagen Sd.Kfz.223 or 'Light Armoured Vehicle Model 223' seen advancing along a road. This armoured car was part of a series of light 4 × 4 armoured reconnaissance 'Aufklärungs' vehicles, and its folding 'bed frame' antennae can be seen fitted onto the main body order to give it both short and long-range radio communication. For local defence, it was armed with a 7.9mm MG34 machine gun. The radio vehicle (Funkwagen) often accompanied other two scout cats to report intelligence.

A StuG.III Ausf.B halted on a road following what appears to have been some fighting action. During the summer of 1941, the StuG acquitted itself very well in its first actions in Ukraine. However, the lack of machine gun for close support against enemy infantry was a problem with early variants.

A Krupp-Protze Kfz.69 hauls a PaK 35/36 through a shallow river bound for the front.

A German infantryman examines a knocked out Russian T-26S tank. While their frontal armour was strong enough to deflect anti-tank fire, German troops were able to outflank and destroy them with explosive charges or point-blank fire.

A Pz.Kpfw.III during operations in western Ukraine in early July 1941. By this time, the battle of the frontier in the Soviet Union was over and armoured and infantry units were pushing forward at speed achieving their tactical bounds, resulting in thousands of Soviet prisoners captured.

A Pz.Kpfw.II, probably an Ausf.F, stands watch over surrendered Russian prisoners. For the opening attack on the Soviet Union, the Panzerwaffe employed some 623 of these tanks.

A column of Pz.Kpfw.IIIs advance through a village. During the first months of the invasion of Ukraine, the Pz.Kpfw.III showed its worth. However, against formidable Russian armour such as the T-34 medium and the KV-1 heavy tanks, the Pz.Kpfw.III was soon recognized as an inadequate weapon in the ranks of the Panzerwaffe.

Two Pz.Kpfw.IIIs, one stationary and the other on the move, can be seen among resting infantry and a field kitchen.

A battery of StuG.IIIs, complete with infantry riding onboard, advance at speed along a dusty road.

A StuG.III Ausf.B advances along a typical dusty road bound for the front. With the vehicles heavy armour and great off-road capability, the StuG could follow the infantry of the Panzergruppen everywhere.

Even by the time the Panzerwaffe invaded Ukraine, much of the motive power on the Eastern Front was animal draught. The bulk of the supplies needed to sustain the German drive were transported by horse, and whilst this helped in many respects, it often curtailed movement. Since both the Infantry and Panzer-Divisions were so reliant on horse transport, units were regularly compelled to stop and wait for the supplies to catch-up. In this photograph, animal draught is hauling a PaK 35/36 anti-tank gun. A typical infantry regiment controlled three battalions, an infantry gun company with six 7.5cm l.IG18 and two 15cm s.IG33 guns, and an anti-tank company with twelve 3.7cm PaK 35/36 guns.

A prime mover can be seen in some undergrowth with what appears to be a 15cm howitzer on tow. The crew have evidently set-up camp and erected a tent from their Zeltbahn shelter quarters and appear to be cooking.

A column of animal draught carrying vital suppliers to the front. Despite the Panzerwaffe's attempts to make their armoured force fully mechanised, a great number of horses were still used throughout the war to carry soldiers and equipment to the front. As a result, many of them perished through physical exertion, hunger, or were killed in battle.

An Sd.Kfz.10 with 2cm FlaK 30 mounted on top leads a column of vehicles through the destroyed city of Kharkov. The sides of the vehicle are up and the national flag can be seen draped over the engine compartment for aerial recognition. The half-track is towing an ammunition trailer.

A Sd.Kfz.7 can be seen towing a chain of supplies along a road. Often animal draught struggled to keep up with the advancing armoured columns. The terrain and bad road systems in Ukraine was also very problematic too.

A prime mover can be seen on the move. It is probably hauling either an 8.8cm Flak gun or 15cm field howitzer to the front.

A half-track prime mover advances along a typically muddy road that has evidently seen a lot of traffic. As with all roads in the Soviet Union, many of them were little more than dirt tracks and were unable to cope with the vast volumes of heavy traffic. When it rained, it hampered movement further with many wheeled vehicles, in particular, becoming stuck.

A column of Sd.Kfz.10 half-tracks have 2cm FlaK 30 mounted on its load-bed, with the drop-sides up for travel. These are Luftwaffe-manned vehicles as evidence by the 'WL' prefix on the front licence plate. These vehicles were issued to Luftwaffe Flakbatteries and their armament was particularly effective against both aerial and ground targets.

Two 18-ton Sd.Kfz.9 prime movers are seen here out on the Russian steppe towing artillery gun carriages. On the Eastern Front, the half-track undoubtedly transformed the fighting ability of artillery and flak batteries to support the advancing armoured spearheads with less difficulty.

A Sd.Kfz.7 half-track leads the way to the frontline followed by a MAN truck full of infantrymen. These infantry vehicles were the most effective method of transportation for troops to reach the front lines without having to march many miles on foot, and then to set up positions and fight.

(**Opposite, above**) A column of German vehicles including an Sd.Kfz.10 half-track with mounted 2cm FlaK 30 gun can be seen passing through the captured town. The extent of damage to the town vividly illustrates the intensity of fighting there had been by the German to capture it.

(**Opposite, below**) Three Sd.Kfz.6/2 half-tracks travel along a road. They all have been mounted with the 3.7cm FlaK 36/37. This vehicle was initially designed as an engineer equipment and personnel carrier, the Mittlerer Zugkraftwagen 5-ton Sd.Kfz.6. It was also deigned to tow artillery and PaK guns, and a variation was produced that mounted a 3.7cm FlaK 36/37 gun. Captured Soviet 7.62cm guns with an armoured rear superstructure were also produced and seen operating on the Eastern Front.

(**Above**) A rear view of a half-track mounted with a FlaK 38 being prepared for a fire-fight against and enemy ground target. Note the drop-sides have been folded down at the rear to allow better access for the crew. A special trailer can be seen attached to the vehicle carrying the bulk of the ammunition.

A stationary Sd.Kfz.10/4 on a dirt road. These half-tracks were designed to carry the 2cm FlaK 30 mount on a special platform with fold downside and rear panels. This platform was specifically designed for the FlaK 30 mount

The crew of an Sd.Kfz.6 rest between some trees and have time to wash and shave before resuming operations. The half-track mounts a 2cm FlaK gun which is protected by the elements by camouflage sheeting. Note the amount of supplies stowed on the platform of the vehicle, including boxes of ammunition. The rear railings have been removed, more than likely for crew access and storage.

The crew of a StuG.III Ausf.B pose for the camera onboard their vehicle during a rest in their advance. Note the letter 'B' painted in white or yellow on the side of the vehicle's superstructure, indicating this was in the second gun battery.

A group of soldiers have taken cover at the rear of a StuG.III. It appears that the soldiers have spotted enemy aircraft activity. The national flag has been draped over the stowage bins that are attached on the engine deck for aerial recognition.

A typical horse-drawn field kitchen. During the drive on Kharkov, and indeed throughout the summer offensive, rations were generally good, but frequently these field kitchens were unable to keep pace with the rapid of advance of the troops. As a consequence, soldiers were compelled to improvise the best they could.

German infantry have taken cover behind a StuG.III during heavy fighting against an enemy position. A Soviet soldier can be seen taken prisoner during the action.

Here, a 1-ton Sd.Kfz.10/4 advances along a road. The half-track mounts a 2cm FlaK anti-aircraft gun. The national flag is attached to the hood of the vehicle for aerial recognition purposes.

Two Pz.Kpfw.IIIs advance through a burning village with infantry using covering fire to pacify remaining enemy resistance without dismounting from the panzers.

Infantry have hitched a lift onboard a column of StuG.III Ausf.B during operations in the summer of 1941. As German forces advanced ever deeper into Ukraine, they encountered stiffer resistance where StuGs and other armoured vehicles became increasingly embroiled in fighting for each village, town and city.

A column of infantry and animal draught carrying vital supplies to the front advance through a city in the summer months of 1941. Note the German national flag draped over the one of the supply wagons for aerial recognition. By mid-1942, such activities were eventually phased out by infantry and armoured crews as they found that the Red Army air force could easily target the vehicles.

A column of hose drawn transport hauling supplies across a bridge bound for the front.

An 8.8cm FlaK gun can be seen mounted on its cruciform gun carriage and being prepared to be used against possible ground targets along a road.

A half-track hauls a 15cm s.FH18 across a river during its onward journey eastwards. This weapon was the standard piece in a division and employment of artillery was a necessity to any ground force engaging an enemy. Both infantry and motorized artillery regiments became the backbone of the fighting in the early years on the Russian front.

A German infantryman stands next to a knocked out BT-7 Russian tank. In the distance, black smoke rises in the air during intense fighting in the area.

(**Above**) An 8-ton Sd.Kfz.7, more than likely part of an artillery regiment attached to a panzer division, rolls through a town.

(**Opposite**) A StuG.III Ausf.B advances along a dusty road. Despite its restrictions with the traverse of its gun, this mobile assault gun continued to be successful at supporting the infantry and exacted a deadly toll on enemy armour as well.

A StuG.III advances along a road. Although this assault gun was seen as an offensive weapon, the lack of close-defence weapons and its light side armour meant that it was not very effective in close-quarters fighting.

Over rough ground, an Sd.Kfz.8 can be seen hauling what appears to be an 8.8cm FlaK gun. This half-track's main role was as a prime mover for heavy towed guns such as the 8.8cm FlaK gun, 21cm Morser 18, the 17cm Kanone 18 17cm, and the 10.5cm gun. It was also very capable of serving as an infantry transport.

A long column of horse-drawn transport crossing a field comprising of infantry equipment, field kitchens and medical supplies. In 1941, there were more than 800,000 horses on the Eastern Front, and by the time winter arrived some 8,000 of them a day were being killed by enemy fire, the extreme arctic temperatures and over exertion. By end of 1941, the Germans were hard-pressed to replenish their supplies of animal draught and were compelled to transport thousands of horses from all over occupied Europe and western Russian.

German infantrymen and a motorcyclist survey the damage wrought to retreating Russian vehicles on a main road.

(**Above**) A very common sight on the Eastern Front, especially after heavy downpour of rain. Particularly in western Russia, the all-weather roads had not been constructed to carry the amount of traffic that now used them, and the surfaces began to break up under the strain. This road has been reduced to a mud track nearly a metre deep and infantrymen have been compelled push the wheeled vehicles through the quagmire.

(**Opposite, above**) A prime mover can be seen crossing a bridge hauling a 15cm howitzer.

(**Opposite, below**) A whitewashed StuG.III has a broken track link and indicates that it's either 'thrown' a track or the track has been damaged by enemy fire. Often the vehicles were moved to one of the Sturmgeschütz workshops in the rear, but the crew appear to be re-tracking in the field, an arduous and labour-intensive job.

During winter operations, crew and infantry negotiate a Pz.Kpfw.III onto a flatbed rail car destined to the front. One of the quickest methods of moving entire panzer divisions to the front was by rail.

A dismounted motorcyclist probably part of the Feldgenarmerie directs a battery of whitewashed StuGs along a road. Even with the high losses of the Sturmgeschütz on the Eastern Front, the crews still had high regard for their self-propelled assault guns as a decisive weapon of war.

Chapter Two

Capture of Ukraine 1942

From his command post Reichenau directed his first battle as commander of Army Group South along the Dnieper River in the area south of Cherkasy, Kremenchuk, Dnepropetrovsk to the eastern banks of Nikopol. It was here, in freezing temperatures, that Army Group South halted strong Soviet attacks and brought the winter offensive in the southern sector to a grinding halt. Both sides were totally exhausted following weeks of ceaseless fighting.

During the cold months of 1942, the Eastern Front stagnated and the Panzerwaffe halted and recuperated from continuous fighting. Even as the Panzerwaffe struggled through the snow from from one position, Hitler was still examining his strategic options despite one of the coldest winters in recorded history. In front of his Generals, he announced to his commanders that the Panzerwaffe and Wehrmacht should be refitted with the utmost speed. Unlike the previous year, he said, when his forces had advanced along three strategic axes toward Moscow, Leningrad and Rostov, they would now concentrate on a drive through the Donets Basin into the bend of the Don River west of Stalingrad and then, south into the oil-rich Caucasus. He confidently revealed that this concerted advance across flat endless landmasses, which were well suited to armoured operations, would ensure the complete encirclements of tens of thousands of Russian troops.

This new bold Operation was codenamed 'Blau' or Blue; this would be the key to the success of the German spearheads through southern Russia, which Hitler said would eventually deprive the resources necessary for the Red Army to continue the war. Subsequently, to achieve these ambitious ends, Hitler sought to blow open the southern front and smash a path for the Wehrmacht to begin its summer offensive through the eastern heartlands of Ukraine using masses of armour and supporting infantry. However, before the operation could be launched, the strategic city of Kharkov had to be captured. Just west of the city, large Red Army formations made a large regrouping effort and began a dual pincer movement from the Volchansk and Barvenkovo salient's. There was a fierce battle with Soviet tank brigades breaking through General Walther Heitz's VIII Corps in the region of Volchansk, which was only 12 miles from Kharkov. What followed was heavy fighting in the area. In fact, the fighting was so fierce that General Paulus's 6th Army lost sixteen battalions in a vain attempt to hold onto its positions. Whilst some armoured units continued to make a series of local counterattacks, the Red Army slowly pushed forward, in spite of serious losses in men and material. Luckily for the Germans, it was clear that in many areas of the front the Russians were weakening. In order to take advantage of the situation, General von Kleist, under the direction of Hitler, ordered his 1st Panzer Army to go onto a counteroffensive.

On 17 May, Kleist's III Panzer Corps and XXXXIV Army Corps launched a large began a large counterattack against the Barvenkovo bridgehead. Parts of the 14th Panzer Division then attacked towards Barvenkovo against the Russian 106th and 341st Rifle Divisions. The 384th Infantry and 16th Panzer Divisions attacked towards Dolgenkaia against the 51st and 335th Rifle Divisions. Supported by aircraft, Kleist's armoured units made a number of deep sweeping attacks and, by the end of the day, parts of the 14th Panzer Division captured Barvenkovo and wrenched opened a 15-mile-wide breach in the Russian defences between Novo Prigozhaia and Barvekovo. Troops and supporting armour then reached the northern Donets River and captured the town of Bogorodichnoye.

On 20 May, the Germans launched a large attack east of Kharkov and, within a few days, successfully linked up with Kleist west of the city, and encircled the main Russian striking force. During the encircling action, the XXI Panzer Corps captured Dzhgun and Krasni Gigant, while to the west the 49th Cavalry Division captured Kirillovka and Voysokii to the north of Krasnograd. The VI Cavalry Corps, supported by the 7th Panzer Brigade, encircled Krasnograd and began to fight for the town.

On 23 May, powerful German armoured formation belonging to Kleist's Panzer Group drove at speed eastwards from the axis of 14th Panzer Division to help seal the outer pocket from escaping enemy forces. The 16th Panzer Division drove at speed west and then north in the direction of Andreevka whilst the 60th Motorized, 384th, 389th and the 100th Light Divisions advanced westwards in order to help seal the pocket. By the end of the day, the 14th Panzer Division re-captured the small town of Chepel whilst simultaneously to the north the 3rd and 23rd Panzer Divisions broke out of their bridgeheads at Andreevka and advanced towards Shebelinka and Kiseli.

As a result of the German armoured formations undertaking large sweeping pincer movements around Kharkov, the Red Army found them encircled near the city. Remnants of the Soviet 317th, 393rd and 150th Rifle, 49th and 26th Cavalry Divisions and the 5th Guards, 7th and 37th Tank Brigades tried, in vain, to break-out. What followed was almost a complete decimate of the Russian pocket.

By early June, some 200,000 Red Army soldiers were killed or captured outside Kharkov. German casualties were specifically lower at 20,000 German dead, wounded or missing. The Russian leadership had undoubtedly underestimated their opponent's strength near the city of Kharkov. As a direct result of their over-confidence, the battle had turned into one of the most catastrophic offensives in Russian military history. The defeat of the Red Army near Kharkov had once more brought invisibility in the eyes of the German commanders, especially to Paulus.

He now believed that the Caucasus was within his grasp, but little did he know what was in store for his forces three months later as it arrived at the banks of the River Volga overlooking the city of Stalingrad.

South of the country, whilst the battle of Khakov had been raging simultaneously, in the Crimea the Germans were making equally good progress. General Manstein's 11th Army had launched a massive counterattack aimed at repulsing Soviet forces from the Kerch area and resuming the offensive on Sevastopol. Opposing the German forces were seventeen infantry divisions, along with several independent brigades. The Germans had seven infantry divisions and a panzer division. Approximately one third of the German force was Romanian. After a number of small attacks in the north, the 11th Army broke through, driving south and pursuing the enemy up to the Kerch straits. Ten days later, on 18 May, the Russians surrendered and 170,000 prisoners fell into German hands.

With the Russians now removed from the Crimea, Manstein was determined more than ever to capture the besieged city of Sevastopol. On 21 May, the Germans launched a massive bombardment on Sevastopol, and for the next few weeks heavy artillery and aircraft attacks pounded the Russian defences. The fortress finally fell on 3 July. Two more Soviet armies had been obliterated and 90,000 prisoners were taken. Hitler, elated at hearing the good news, phoned von Manstein and commended him as 'The Conqueror of Sevastopol', informing him that he had ordered von Manstein's promotion to General Field Marshal.

Following the fall of Sevastopol, the caves that surrounded Ukraine were almost entirely under German control. The rapid German advance had led to the destruction or partial destruction of the country with much of its industrial base in ruins. Yet, the German triumph over Ukraine would be short-lived. Further to the southeast of the country, along the Volga River, the 6th Army had become perilously embroiled in what became known as the Battle of Stalingrad. By the end of 1942, the army was encircled, but held out until the end of January 1943, when it finally surrendered. There was a complete and dramatic reversal of fortune for the German Army in the south. With Stalingrad lost, many parts of the German front simply caved-in as the Red Army's Central Front turned its attention west, expanding its offensive against both Army Group South and Army Group Centre. In February, the front had moved almost 200 miles in less than ten weeks, threatening German forces in eastern Ukraine and the strategically important city of Kharkov. As German units retreated, they were instructed under Hitler's orders to create 'a zone of annihilation'. Everything was to be destroyed in their wake. Stiff resistance by the Germans managed to eventually slow the Soviet drive and this included a determined effort by Field Marshal Manstein Erich launching his Kharkov counterstrike. What followed was the Battle of Kharkov. By 15 March, the Germans had recaptured the city and two days later recaptured Belgorod, creating the salient which, in July 1943, would lead to the Battle of Kursk. Ukraine was now under imminent Russian threat.

Winter clad panzergrenadiers can be seen on the advance crossing a snowy plane supported by a whitewashed Pz.Kpfw.III.

A column of Pz.Kpfw.IIIs cross a wooden bridge during winter operations. During the summer and winter of 1941, the Pz.Kpfw.III was, numerically, the most important panzer operating on the frontline. During this period, the majority of available tanks including re-armed Ausf.E and F variants and the additional new Ausf.G and H models were armed with the 5cm KwK 38 L/42 50mm cannon.

A column of panzers pass through a village. Two Pz.Kpfw.IVs lead the drive and a whitewashed Pz.Kpfw.II follows behind.

A panzer crew are rests on their vehicle during a halt in their advance during early winter operations. Three crew members utilise a Zeltbahn shelter quarter to help combat the biting wind and cold.

In the snow a Sd.Kfz.232 (Fu) (8 Rad) – reconnaissance armoured vehicle with a 2cm cannon and Fu 12 radio station with frame-type antenna. This model was very distinctive because of the heavy 'bedspring' antenna over most of the hull.

Infantrymen converse in front of a support vehicle during the early winter of 1942.

A column of non-armoured vehicles, some of which are hauling ordinance, advance along a road that has seen a lot of heavy traffic. Often a light downpour of rain could turn these roads into a quagmire halting an advance.

During a reconnaissance mission Russian troops have been captured and questioned. On the left of the photograph is an Sd.Kfz.251/3 half-track complete with frame antenna. On the right is an Sd.Kfz.250/3 radio vehicle. This vehicle was used widely during the war and was designed as a basic troop carrier and for reconnaissance units which carried scout sections. This basic variant was usually armed with one or two MG34 machine guns. Later variants carried 2cm, 3.7cm and even 7.5cm cannons to support other armoured units and lighting armoured vehicles.

A column of prime movers hauling 15cm howitzers are seen halted on a road. On the opposite side of the road is a line of stationary support vehicles.

Spread out purposely across a field in order to minimise damage, if this armoured regiment was attacked, various vehicles can be seen stationary, some of which are concealed by foliage.

A pioneer unit can be seen erecting a bridge across a river with the assistance of half-track prime movers. Pioneers were regarded as a separate combat arm which was specifically trained in construction and the demolition of fortifications. However, they were often used as specialist infantry, serving the role of combat engineers. One battalion was assigned to each Corps.

A Sd.Kfz.10/5 half-track driving across uneven ground but showing its versatility. This vehicle saw extensive use during the Second World War. Initially, its main role was as a prime mover for small, towed guns, such as the 2cm FlaK 30, the 7.5cm leIG, or the 3.7cm PaK 36 anti-tank gun. It could carry eight troops in addition to towing a gun or trailer. This half-track has been converted into self-propelled anti-flak vehicle and mounts the 2cm FlaK 38 gun. It is towing an ammunition trailer.

Two photographs showing Sturmartillerie uniforms. In 1940, these uniforms were introduced for both Sturmartillerie and Panzerjäger units. The uniform was specially designed primarily to be worn inside and away from their armoured vehicles; for this reason designers had produced a garment that gave better camouflage qualities than the standard black Panzer uniform. The uniform worn by units of the Panzerjäger was made entirely from lightweight grey-green wool material. The cut was very

similar to that of the black Panzer uniform. However, it did differ in respect of insignia and the collar patches. The Panzerjäger uniform was a very practical garment and it was identical to the cut of the to the Sturmartillerie uniform, but with the exception of the colour. The uniform was made entirely of field-grey cloth but again differed in respect to certain insignia. The collar patches consisted of the death's head emblems, which were stitched on patches of dark blue-green cloth and were edged with bright rcd Waffcnfarbc piping.

A Sd.Kz.10/4 half-track mounting a 2cm FlaK 30. All the crew wear the universally supplied Zeltbahn shelter quarters to protect themselves from the elements. Note the weight of the vehicle painted in white letters beside the driver's compartment.

A half-track can be seen stationary next to two well-supplied halted StuG.IIIs. Behind these vehicles are infantry with animal draught more than likely hauling ordinance or supplies. Often the vehicles outstripped their supply columns.

Sd.Kfz.10 half-tracks hauling 5cm PaK 38 ordnance towards the battle front. In the distance, a battery of 15cm field howitzers are preparing for a fire mission. This weapon was the standard piece in a division and employment of artillery was a necessity to any ground force engaging an enemy. Both infantry and motorized artillery regiments became the backbone of the fighting in the early years on the Eastern Front. The 15cm field howitzer was primarily designed to attack targets deeper into the enemy rear. This included command posts, reserve units, assembly areas, and logistic facilities.

A stationary Pz.Kpfw.III using a building as cover against enemy ground or aerial recognition.

An Sd.Kfz.251/5 Schützenpanzerwagen für Pionierzug or Assault Engineer vehicle can be seen. Early command vehicles for Pioneer platoons (Pionierzug) such as this one were equipped with the Pak 35/36 gun mount. Note the pioneer mortar crew in action showing the 8cm sGrW 34 mortar being fired against an enemy target. Each battalion fielded six 8cm sGrW 34 mortars.

What appears to be Pz.Kpfw.IIIs halted inside a wooded area or order to conceal its regiments' movement from enemy aerial recognition.

An Sd.Kfz.10 has halted in a field whilst the crew prepare for a fire mission. The Sd.Kfz.10 was primarily designed to tow light ordnance such as 2cm and 3.7cm PaK, 5cm PaK 38 guns and 7.5cm artillery pieces, as well. It was also used to mount 2cm FlaK guns.

Infantry can be seen advancing along the side a road towards the battlefront. A column of various vehicles including a motorcycle combination have halted on the opposite side of the road.

Two crew members survey the terrain ahead through a pair of binoculars onboard a Pz.Kpfw.III. Note the wooden logs festooned to the engine deck to assist the crew when the tank was negotiating uneven or boggy terrain.

Pz.Kpfw.IIIs on the advance complete with infantry which at a movements notice could dismount and go into action. The divisional insignia is painted in yellow on the right panzer. This indicates the tanks belong to the 14th Panzer Division. In early 1942, the division took part in the German summer offensives as Army Group South advanced through the Kharkov and Don areas. It was later transferred to the VI Army, which then became encircled Stalingrad. By February 1943, the division was destroyed fighting in what became known as the Battle of Stalingrad.

A very common scene during the German Army's march through Ukraine. Animal draught and supply vehicles are on the move across endless miles of dusty roads.

A long column of Pz.Kpfw.IIIs on the advance along a muddy road. A log has been attached to the vehicle to help the crew combat the boggy and uneven terrain. One log was often enough to be placed under one of the tracks to give the vehicle traction.

Half-tracks carrying troops towards the battlefront. These Sd.Kfz.250 series vehicles, with a command variant on the right, belong to the 13th Panzer-Division. The division contributed to the successful encirclements of the Red Army at Kyiv in 1941. It was attached to Army Group South Ukraine, which had orders to stop the Soviets from capturing the Romanian oil fields. The division was later reformed in July 1944 and was upgraded with newer panzers such as the Panther Ausf.G and Jadpanzer IV.

A Pz.Kpfw.III churns up dust clouds as it races across a field during summer operations.

An 8-ton Sd.Kfz.7 tows an 8.8cm FlaK 36 or 37 through a shallow river. By 1942, this deadly 8.8cm Flak gun was used extensively both against ground and aerial targets. Throughout the war in Ukraine, the supply situation was exacerbated by the almost non-existence of proper road. Half-tracks and other tracked vehicles were utilized to help speed up the supply of ammunition and other equipment desperately required for the front.

An interesting photograph showing an infantryman repairing a vehicle whilst an Sd.Kfz.8 tows a broken-down Pz.Kpfw.IV to a maintenance workshop.

A Panzer crew are seen securing a Pz.Kpfw.IV on a flatbed rail car. During 1942, especially in Ukraine, the Panzerwaffe found that moving often whole panzer divisions by rail from one part of the front to another, was the quickest method of achieving success along the front.

Several stationary Pz.Kpfw.IV during operations in the summer of 1942. Note the 'K' painted on the left Pz.Kpfw.IV Ausf.D. This indicates that these vehicles belonged to Army Group Kleist after its commander General Paul Ludwig von Kleist. During the summer of 1942 Army Group South subdivided into Army Group A and B. Army Group A, which included Kleist's 1st Panzer Army, had the task of leading the Axis thrust into the Caucasus.

Panzer commanders converse with maps during their advance during early winter operations.

Chapter Three

Fighting Withdrawal 1943

The reverberations caused by the defeat at Kursk meant that German forces in the south bore the brunt of the heaviest Soviet drive. Both the Russian Voronezh and Steppe Fronts possessed massive local superiority against everything the Germans had on the battlefield, and this included their diminishing resources of tanks and assault guns. The Panzerwaffe were now duty-bound to improvise with what they had at their disposal and try to maintain themselves in the field; in doing so, they hoped to wear the enemy's offensive capacity. But in the south, where the weight of the Soviet effort was directed, Army Group South's line began breaking and threatened to be ripped wide open. Stiff defensive action was now the stratagem placed upon the Panzerwaffe, but they lacked sufficient reinforcements and the strength of their armoured units dwindled steadily as they tried to hold back the Russian might.

During the first uneasy weeks of August 1943, the 1st Panzer Army and Armeeabteilung Kempf fought to hold ground along the Donets River whilst the final battle of Kharkov was fought. Further north, near the battered town of Akhtyrka, the 4th Panzer Army was fighting a frenzied battle of attrition. Along the whole Russian front, massive Soviet artillery bombardments would sweep the German lines inflicting considerable casualties on infantry and armoured vehicles. Throughout August and September, the Panzerwaffe tried frantically to hold on to a receding front line. With just over 1,000 Panzers operating in southern Russia, the Germans were seriously under strength and still further depleted by vehicles being constantly taken out for repair. Along many areas of the front, high losses resulted from inadequate supplies and not the skill of the defenders.

In other areas of the Russian front, the situation was just the same. Both Army Group Centre and Army Group North were trying desperately to hold the Soviets back from breaking through their lines. Replacements continued to trickle through to help bolster the weakened Panzerwaffe. But in truth, the average new Panzer soldier that was freshly recruited was not as well trained as his predecessors during the early part of the campaign in Russia. Nevertheless, as with many Panzer men, they were characterized by high morale and a determination to do their duty.

In nearly three months since the defeat at Kursk, Army Centre and South had been pushed back an average distance of 150 miles on a 650-mile front. Despite heavy resistance in many sectors of the front, the Soviets lost no time in exploiting the fruits of regaining as much territory as possible. In Army Group South, where the frontlines threatened to completely cave in under intense enemy pressure, frantic appeals to Hitler were made by Field Marshal Manstein to withdraw his forces across the Dnieper River. There was a fighting withdrawal that degenerated into a race with the Russians for possession of the river. Army Group South, which comprised of the 1st and 4th Panzer Army and included 2,400 tanks, was given the ambitious task of trying to hold positions along the Dnieper River which resulted in the Battle of the Dnieper. Manstein had to defend the river against the powerful Belorussian, 1st, 2nd, 3rd, and 4th Ukrainian Fronts, which had one of the largest concentrations of men and armour distributed along the Eastern Front. In order to try and hold back the overwhelming fire power of the Red Army, the Panzer divisions were ordered to cover the rear, whilst the army group's columns slowly withdrew on selected river crossing points at Cherkassy, Dniepropetrovsk, Kyiv, Kanev and Krmenchug, leaving behind a burnt a blasted wasteland during their retreat.

The crossing of the Dnieper River, before the battered and worn front disintegrated into total ruin, was one of the major achievements of Field Marshal von Manstein's career. The Germans still believed they could stabilize the front, but the Soviet numerical superiority was far too great. By trying to hold the east side of the Dnieper, the Germans had sapped most of the strength out of Army Group South and Centre. The Panzerwaffe was now required to try and perform yet another reversal of Germany's misfortunes in Ukraine. In most areas of the front, Panzer crews were no longer to adopt any risky offensive tactics but to use a delaying and blocking strategy instead. As the third winter fast approached, they hoped that the arctic conditions would also impede the onset of another Russian offensive.

The winter of 1943 opened up with an exasperating series of deliberations for the Panzerwaffe in Ukraine. Much of its concerns were preventing the overwhelming might of the Red Army with what little armoured support they had available at their disposal. By 15 October, the Russian 2nd Ukrainian Front had crossed the Dnieper River. During the next few days, it poured divisions across the river and wrenched open the German held front between the 8th Army and the left wing of the 1st Panzer Army. The city of Krivoi Rog was then under threat of being attacked and captured. Manstein knew how important to the city was to his Army Group and it stored the supply and ammunition dumps for the area, and the locomotives there were a vital asset for the supply to his forces. In order to defend the city, Manstein scraped together six weakened armoured divisions including elite Waffen-SS Division 'Totenkopf'. However, although fighting was difficult, Panzers units managed to knock out some 300 Red Army tanks and forced the Russians to withdraw back towards the Dnieper River. Manstein knew this success was only temporary. The situation along the Dnieper River was bleak. By mid-to late October, Red Army formations began drawing German forces away from both the Lower Dnieper and from the city of Kyiv.

As the winter set-in the front stagnated again, but by December, Red Army forces controlled a bridgehead almost 200-miles wide and 60-miles deep in a number of areas. In the south, the Crimea was now cut-off from the rest of the German forces and any success of blocking Red Army formations from advancing from the east bank of the Dnieper had been lost forever.

By early November, despite the harsh weather conditions, the Russians had once more begun to roll across the wet and snowy plains of the western parts of Ukraine. In the wake of a massive artillery bombardment, Soviet forces hit the centre of the German front with such a force it ripped it open. In just two days, the 4th Panzer Army front around Lutezh collapsed. During the night of 5 November, the battle swept through Kyiv, and the next morning Panzers supported by infantry retreated. Lacking reserves of any kind, armoured vehicles of the 4th Panzer Army were helpless as it tried to defend the rear of its forces. For the next two weeks, a bitter and bloody battle raged.

On 20 November, the 1st Panzer Army, which had been fighting continuously for days in the region around Nikopol, reported to the Army Group that their strength had sunk to the lowest tolerable level. Gloomy as the situation was, armoured units were compelled to try and fill the gaps left by the infantry and hold the front to the grim death. Throughout December, the Panzerwaffe fought well, and at times even succeeded surprising Red Army forces with a number of daring attacks of their own. Manstein was fully aware of the strategic importance of the right bank of Ukraine and Crimea. Despite the deep snow and treacherous weather conditions, in order to defend large parts of the right bank of the river and ensure troops could be protected on the Crimea peninsula, Army Group South and Army Group A put together two panzer and two field armies, from north to south. It was supported by both Hungarian and Romanian forces. In total, there were some 93 divisions including eighteen panzer and four panzergrenadier divisions, two motorized brigades, three heavy panzer battalions of Tiger tanks, eighteen Sturmgeschütz Assault Gun Brigades, a battalion of 'Elefant' tank destroyers, a mixture of artillery and PaK battalions, including pioneer engineering units. Almost half of the German troops, and three-quarters of the Panzerwaffe that were employed on the Eastern Front were to take part in the defence of the west bank of Ukraine. The Dnieper-Carpathian Offensive followed and would involve some 3.5 million troops stretching some 800-miles in length. The offensive was to be the first and only time during the entire war on the Eastern Front that six Soviet armies and elite mechanized armoured formations would be used, at once, in a single battle.

On Christmas Eve 1943, the offensive was launched by the 1st Ukrainian Front against the German 4th Army to the west and southwest of Kyiv. All along the front, Russian units comprising of masses of tanks and self-propelled guns crashed into action. The Red Army assaults were so powerful that infantry and armoured divisions soon surrounded Kyiv and quickly recaptured Zhitomir. West of Zhitomir, heavy unrelenting fighting engulfed the German lines knocking out heavy tanks such as Panther and Tiger Is. Although Manstein's armoured units managed to hold on to parts of the disintegrating front, the majority of German units had already been pushed back some 100 miles. Their fighting withdrawal had proven to be successful but was a temporary measure. Although Hitler had ordered that every man was not to withdraw from his position and fight where he stood, the German withdrawal was a tactical retreat in order to save the complete destruction of his forces in Ukraine.

(**Below**) A column of whitewashed StuG.IIIs advance through the snow during early winter operations in 1943. By this period of the war, the StuG had become a very popular assault gun, especially on the Eastern Front. Its low profile and mechanical reliability saw their employment grow on the battlefield. Some 3,041 of them were operational in 1943 alone on the Eastern Front.

(**Opposite, above**) A prime mover hauls an 8.8cm flak gun through a snowy village.

(**Opposite, below**) The second version of the Marder.II was known as the Panzerkampwagen II als Sfl. Mit 7.5cm PaK 40 'Marder II' (Sd.Kfz.131) is seen during the winter. This tank hunter was based on a modified Pz.Kpfw.II Ausf.F tank chassis. Its design comprised of converting the tank and mounting a PaK 40 on the tank chassis. Production of these vehicles began at the same time as the first version of the Marder.II.

Two photographs showing Waffen-SS Sd.Kfz.251/10 Ausf.C armed with a 3.7cm PaK 36 advancing through the recaptured city of Kharkov. On 12 March 1943, the SS-Leibstandarte fought through stiff Red Army defences in the northern suburbs of the city and began a house-to-house fight towards the centre. The next day, the SS fought house to house clearing out all Soviet resistance and effectively captured Kharkov on 14 March with the assistance of elements of the SS-Das Reich Division which was still fighting in the southern part of the city.

Prime mover can be seen towing a trailer full of supplies including bridging sections and a motorcycle.

A crewmember can be seen with a Marder.II. These vehicles were used to equip both infantry and Panzer divisions and were seen operating in both Wehrmacht and Waffen-SS anti-tank companies. The Marder.II was used mainly on the Eastern Front, and the majority were sent to southern Russian in Ukraine during the summer of 1942, where many of them were lost in battle.

(**Above**) A column of half-tracks towing a battery of 15cm field howitzers have halted on a road.

(**Opposite, above**) An Sd.Kfz.10/4 with 2cm FlaK 30 in a field. By 1942 German anti-tank and flak units were compelled to try and fill the gaps left by the infantry and hold the front at whatever cost in men and material. During 1942 and the first half of 1943 self-propelled anti-tanks and aircraft units fought well and were regarded a significant contribution to the overstretched Panzerwaffe. During this period of the war, there was much innovation adapting and converting tank chassis and half-tracks. There had been the introduction of the Sd.Kfz.10/5 FlaK 38; the Sd.Kfz.7 half-track was also converted into a number of self-propelled anti-aircraft variants using both the 2cm and 3.7cm flak guns. The Sd.Kfz.7/1 was converted and mounted the powerful 2cm Flakvierling 38 quadruple flak gun. The Sd.Kfz.7/2 variant was armed with a single 3.7cm FlaK 36 anti-aircraft gun. There were also numerous conversions made mounting a single 2cm anti-aircraft gun.

(**Opposite, below**) The crew of the new Marder.III series prepare to re-arm its vehicle in a field. This third version of the Marder was to see action on the Eastern Front and was known as the *Panzerjäger 38(t) für 7.62cm PaK 36(r) 'Marder III'* (Sd.Kfz.139). The Germans used obsolete tank chassis utilizing the old Pz.Kpfw.38(t) tank. The design comprised of removing the under gunned 3.7cm KwK 38(t) gun and turret and replacing it with the Soviet 7.62cm PaK 36(r). Manufacturing of the *Panzerjäger* 38(t) Marder.III went into production at the end of March 1942, and within weeks the vehicle saw its debut with the *Wehrmacht* and *Waffen-SS* on the Eastern Front. Crews soon reported its tactical worth, as it was more than capable of destroying Soviet T-34 tank. These tank hunters extensively served with the divisional anti-tank battalions and proved very successful at countering Russian armour in Ukraine. Between 1942 and 1944 some 1,500 Marder.IIIs were produced.

Sd.Kfz.6 pioneer vehicles can be seen towing bridging sections next to the Dnieper River. These poineerwagen typically towed trailer loads comprising of medium pontoons and light pontoons for pioneers. These half-tracks were often seen at the riverbank during bridge erections before assault teams stormed the bridge.

Panzergrenadiers have dismounted from a stationary Sd.Kfz.251. One soldier can be seen next to a building armed with a Stg.24 stick grenade and is poised to throw it through the window.

Two Sd.Kfz.251 half-tracks support two Pz.Kpfw.II and a Pz.Kpfw.III during operations near the Dnieper River. By this period of the war in Ukraine, the Panzerwaffe were fighting a withdrawal that degenerated into a race with the Russians for possession of the river. Whilst the Panzer divisions covered the rear, columns of troops withdrew on selected river crossing points at Cherkassy, Dniepropetrovsk, Kyiv, Kanev, and Krmenchug, leaving behind a burnt wasteland during their retreat.

A StuG.III can be seen being re-supplied with ammunition. By 1943, the Panzerwaffe were increasingly hard-pressed as the Soviet war machine was applying newer technology to compete against the German assault guns.

(**Opposite, above**) A StuG.III Ausf.G whilst operating in Ukraine. Though the Germans required more assault guns to combat the growing menace of the Red Army, production of the Ausf.G was initially curtailed due to heavy allied air raids on the factories. However, in spite of the problems, many Ausf.G variants were still to appear in Ukraine as formidable weapons of war.

(**Opposite, below**) The crew of a StuG.III rest during a lull in the fighting. Throughout the mid war years, the assault gun provided crucial mobile fire support to the infantry and it also proved its worth as an invaluable anti-tank vehicle.

(**Opposite, above**) A column of Pz.Kpfw.III rolls through a town during its unit's withdrawal. Despite the dire situation on the Eastern Front, the Panzerwaffe still believed they could stabilize the front, but Soviet numerical superiority was far too great. By trying to hold the east side of the Dnieper, the Germans had sapped most of the strength out of Army Group South and Centre. In most areas of the front, Panzers crews were no longer to adopt any risky offensive tactics but to use a delaying and blocking strategy instead. As the third winter fast approached, they hoped that the arctic conditions would also impede the onset of another Russian offensive.

(**Above**) An excellent photograph showing StuG.III destined for the front. Note the canvas cover to protect the crew compartment from the rain.

(**Opposite**) Two photographs showing a Tiger tank during summer operations. Although these tanks were undoubtedly formidable fighting machines whose arrival at the front was a welcomed relief to the already hard-pressed Panzerwaffe, there were too few of them delivered to the front. Instead, Tigers, Panthers, assault guns and tank destroyer crews found that they were too thinly stretched to make any considerable dent against the growing tank might of the Red Army.

A column of Tiger tanks with infantry hitching a lift can be seen during winter operations.

Two photographs showing gunners seen preparing the new self-propelled converted vehicle nicknamed the Hummel for a fire mission. Initially, this vehicle was called 'bumblebee'. It was designated as Panzerfeldhaubitze 18M auf Geschützwagen III/IV (Sf) Hummel, Sd.Kfz.165. It mounted the powerful 15cm sFH 18 L/30 howitzer on the specially converted chassis of a Pz.Kpfw.III/IV. The Hummel's 15cm HE high explosive shells came in two parts. The explosive shell was loaded first, followed by the variable charge canister. As a result of this firing procedure, the Hummel could only carry eighteen rounds of shells. Expenditure of ammunition could often be quick if the battle was on-going and for this reason the Hummel included an ammunition carrying Munitionsträger. On the battlefield, they were formed into separate, heavy, self-propelled artillery batteries, each with six Hummel and a Munitionsträger.

(**Opposite, above**) Two whitewashed Tiger tanks advance along a snowy road. The mighty Tiger's played a key role in operations in Ukraine between 1943 and 1944.

(**Opposite, below**) Winter-clad panzergrenadiers can be seen with a stationary whitewashed Tiger. The reason for the survival of many of these Tigers on the battlefield was due to its heavy armoured plating, which was more resistant to combat damage than other lighter tanks. In addition, Tiger tank battalions often had well equipped maintenance companies who could return these heavy tanks to the battlefield swiftly.

(**Above**) Infantrymen stand next to an Sd.Kfz.6 during a pause in battle. All of the soldiers wear the distinctive reversible parka grey side out.

(**Above**) Two winter-clad soldiers pose for the camera next to a VW type 82 'Kubelwagen'.

(**Opposite, above**) A photograph taken in 1943 showing a 15cm sIG 33(Sf.) auf Pz.Kpfw.38(t) 'Grille' Ausf.M (Cricket), (Sd.Kfz.138/1). The superstructure of this vehicle was built around the sIG 33 howitzer, which was open-top. Its design made the crew vulnerable to enemy fire. The majority of the ammunition was stored on the superstructure walls due to restricted space, while other rounds stored in the hull. They were produced in limited numbers and service on all fronts and were assigned to panzergrenadier regiments. Although the vehicles had disadvantages, the Wehrmacht were able to field fast-moving 15cm field howitzers along the front. As with all self-propelled artillery, the vehicles had the tactical ability to fire off a round and then quickly relocate to another position with encountering any expected return fire.

(**Below**) Winter-clad panzergreandiers are being supported by a whitewashed Marder.II. Despite its vulnerability out in the field, this Panzerjäger was a very effective weapon, especially during defensive roles, where it was employed more and more.

A whitewashed Tiger tank supports panzergrenadiers during winter operations. As desperation gripped the battered and bruised front lines in Ukraine, troops became much more reliant on both the Tiger and Panther for defence. Since 1942, the Tiger had dominated the battlefield on the Eastern Front. By late 1943, there were never enough available in sufficient numbers in the defensive battles, yet they still played a key role. Again and again, these armoured monsters demonstrated their awesome killing power, playing a prominent position in the defence against numerically superior Soviet armoured forces. But with the tide turned against the Panzerwaffe, they were overstretched and slowly destroyed.

Chapter IV

Lost Battles 1944

The new year for the Panzerwaffe in Ukraine opened up with a frustrating series of withdrawals and fighting from one decimated position to another. In the first week of January, Russian armoured formations had advanced to a depth of nearly 60 miles, completely clearing German forces from the Kyiv and Zhytomyr regions, including a number of districts in and around Vinnitsa and Rovno. As the front quickly begun to crack under the sheer weight of the Soviet attacks on 5 January, the 2nd Ukrainian Front launched what was known as the Kirovograd Offensive. One of its first objectives was to stem the III Panzer Corps attacks which were being used as blocking unit in the Kirovograd region. What followed, was a series of large-scale Red Army attacks. Losses to both German troops and armour were massive. In spite of the repeated requests by Manstein to Hitler for permission to withdraw, fighting continued and losses mounted. This culminated in the decimation of the III Panzer Corps and the loss of the town of Kirovograd. With the loss of the town, the front further crumbled and Manstein quickly pulled together Some eleven German divisions, including the SS Division 'Wiking' division and the new Belgian Walloon volunteer unit, SS 'Sturmbrigade Wallonien', were ordered to stem the Soviet drive westwards. Here these strong German divisions comprising of well-seasoned troops and numerous heavy panzers and self-propelled guns were to hold a salient into the Soviet lines between the towns of Korsun and Cherkassy. On 18 January, Vatutin's 1st and Konev's 2nd Ukrainian Fronts then attacked the salient and surrounded two German corps. Trapped in what was known as the 'Korsun pocket' were some 50,000 men, a total of six German divisions, including the elite SS 'Wiking' and the SS 'Sturmbrigade Wallonien'. The 'Wiking' division was the only armoured unit in the pocket with some forty-three tanks and assault guns. Two assault gun battalions provided an additional twenty-seven assault guns. With these tanks and assault guns, they were ordered to drive the strong Russian forces back and break out of the encirclement and destroy the enemy. Over the next few days fighting raged with huge casualties being inflicted on the German units trying to break out. As the situation further deteriorated, the 1st SS Panzer- Division 'Leibstandarte' was hurried to the area in order to relieve the pocket. Oberstleutnant Franz Bake's Tiger tanks of the 503.Schwere-Panzer-Abteilung, was then sent at speed to open the pocket. Despite the assistance of Baker's Tigers, his tanks and supporting vehicles found the terrain almost impassable as the winter thaw had come early and turned the terrain in to a quagmire. Nonetheless, deep in mud the SS tanks supported by Wehrmacht units continued fighting its way through. By 8 February, parts of the 'Leibstandarte' and 16th Panzer-Division had reached and established bridgeheads across the Gniloi Tickich River, west of Boyarka. The encircled troops known as 'Gruppe Stemmerman' began withdrawing forces from the north of the pocket and attacking south towards the relief forces on the north bank of the Gniloi Tickich.

On 16 February, Hitler finally gave the order to break out of the pocket. As troops and remaining armoured units broke out, they were engulfed by a massive barrage of heavy artillery causing massive casualties. There were enormous losses in men and equipment, yet some 33,000 German troops had escaped the pocket. The battle and relief effort meant that more than 70,000 men were killed, captured and wounded. Outside the pocket, the 1st Panzer Army had lost 300 tanks and assault guns. Although the losses were huge in Manstein's eyes, another major disaster that had been averted in Ukraine.

During the remainder of February, the Soviet offensive continued grinding further west. At the beginning of March 1944, Army Group A and South still held about half the ground between the Dnieper and Bug, but in a number of areas the front was buckling under the constant strain of repeated Soviet attacks. As a consequence, Army Group South was being slowly pressed westwards, its Panzers still unable to strike a decisive counter-blow because of the Führer's order to stand fast on unsuitable positions. By 24 March, the Russians had spearheaded to the Dniester, and a few days later were penetrating the foothills of the Carpathians. Panzerwaffe units that were refused by Hitler to withdraw found themselves tied down trying in vain to hold back the Soviet avalanche. These battles became known to the Panzer soldiers as the 'cauldron battles' or Kesselschlachten.

By April, mud finally brought an end to almost continuous fighting in the south, and there was respite for the Panzerwaffe in some areas of the front. Once more, despite the setbacks, there was a genuine feeling of motivation within the ranks of the Panzerwaffe. There was renewed determination to use numerous armoured blocking units in western Ukraine to hold-back the Red Army assaults. In addition, confidence was further bolstered by the efforts of the armaments industry as they begun producing many new vehicles for the Eastern Front. In fact, during 1944, the Panzerwaffe were better supplied with equipment during any other time on the Eastern Front, thanks to the armaments industry. In total, some 20,000 fighting vehicles including 8,328 medium and heavy tanks, 5,751 assault guns, 3,617 tank destroyers and 1,246 self-propelled artillery carriages of various types reached the Eastern Front. Included in these new arrivals were the second generation of tank-destroyers, the Jagdpanzer IV, followed by the Hetzer and then the Jagpanther and Jagdtiger. Tank-destroyers and assault guns would soon outnumber the tanks, which was confirmation of the Panzerwaffe's obligation to performing a defensive role against overwhelming opposition. All of these vehicles would have to be irrevocably stretched along a very thin Eastern Front, with many of them rarely reaching the proper operating level. Panzer divisions too were often broken up and split among hastily constructed battle groups or Kampfgruppe drawn from a motley collection of armoured formations. Regardless, these battle groups were put into the line operating well below strength. The demands that were put upon the Panzerwaffe during the spring of 1944 in Ukraine were immeasurable. The constant employment, coupled with the nightmare of not having enough supplies, was a growing worry among the tank commanders.

Slowly and inexorably, the Soviets continued driving its powerful units eastwards. In April, the Russian 2nd Guards Army had broken south through the Perekop isthmus into the western regions of Ukraine in what the Red Army called the Crimea Offensive Operation. For a number of months, the German 17th Army had been trapped in the Crimea with Hitler determined to hold onto the peninsula at all costs. It would not be until 3 May that Hitler would order the evacuation of the Crimea. Some 130,000 men were evacuated by sea and 21,000 by air. Out of the total strength of 560 panzer and assault guns, less than a quarter was salvaged with many vehicles either abandoned or destroyed during combat. The losses were huge, and there were no replacements.

Further north along the Dnieper River, fighting was still raging. Field Marshal Walter Model, who had replaced Manstein after he was sacked at the end of March 1944, was given the enormous task of trying to minimize the extent of the disaster on the west bank of the Dnieper. Mainstein's Army Group North Ukraine comprised of two Panzer armies and the 1st Hungarian Army. Some 420 tanks and self-propelled guns with various other vehicles were thrown together. However, as Model prepared his force to be used as a kind of blocking army group in Ukraine, the Russians on 22 June launched 'Operation Bagration' directed at the German central front. Within days, the German front began to cave-in and Model was called to Army Group Centre in order to salvage the deteriorating situation. Model was replaced by General Josef Harper. Harper was fully aware of the dire consequences in Ukraine if they were defeated. They appreciated that if the Red Army succeeded here then it would undoubtedly wrench wide open the door to Poland and the Homeland. Hitler told his frontline commanders that the German forces must improve their present positions and stand and fight. Since March 1944, Hitler had been obsessed with his new 'Fester Platz' or 'Fortified Area' order. These fortified areas were established in a number of main Russian and Ukrainian towns and cities and manned by strong German armoured and troop formations; they were ordered to stem the Red Army onslaught by using various degrees of fanatical defence. Although these defences were relatively effective in holding back some Russian units, the German fortified areas were often bypassed by Red Army troops leaving the Germans encircled and trapped.

The situation in Ukraine was made more difficult for the German defenders when, on 13 July, the 1st Ukrainian Front launched a massive attack signalling the Lvov-Sandomierz offensive. The offensive was aimed towards the city of Lwow. Taking the initial brunt of the attacks was the 1st and 4th Panzer Divisions. The

German 357th Infantry Division, 349th Infantry Division, the SS-Freiwillge Division 'Galizien' and the III.Panzer Corps along with the 8th Panzer-Division were brought-up to try and stem the massive Red Army onslaught towards Lwow.

The Russian offensive was overwhelming and within days Red Army units including the 3rd Guards Tank Army managed to encircle 45,000 men of the XIII Army Corps, which were trapped around Brody. There were a number of desperate attempts by under-strength and exhausted Panzer units to relieve the Brody cauldron, but the men inside were trapped and help was futile. As a result of this encirclement, a 170-mile breach had been created along the Army Group North Ukraine's front. In order to avoid complete annihilation, German troops and armour were quickly withdrawn from the breach. However, the scene was one of complete chaos and destruction as German columns fell-back. The 4th Panzer Army retreated towards the Vistula River and the 1st Panzer Army along with 1st Hungarian Army withdrew to the area around the Carpathian Mountains and held the city of Lwow.

On 24 July, the 1st Panzer Army set-up defensive positions around the city of Lwow with its front to the south. However, panzer crews had neither the man-power, weapons, panzers or enough assault guns to effectively fight for the city. As a result, two days later overwhelming Russian forces began advancing into the suburbs. What was left of the 1st Panzer Division begun withdrawing to avoid complete decimation. The city fell with relative ease.

With the capture of Lwow, the situation in western Ukraine quickly deteriorated for the Germans. As a result, many panzer and troops formations were forced out of Ukraine where many began regrouping in Poland.

(**Opposite, above**) Tiger and Panther tanks can be seen operating across the frozen plains west of the Dnieper River in the early winter. With the east bank of the Dnieper more or less seized by the Red Army commanders were preparing plans for what they called, 'the liberation of right-bank Ukraine'. What followed was a huge offensive with the sole objective of crushing German troops and armoured positions from the Dnieper to the Carpathians, from Polsia to the Black Sea, encompassing the right-bank of Ukraine, Western Ukraine, Crimea and even parts of Moldova and Romania.

(**Opposite, below**) Whitewashed Tiger tanks being replenished with supplies out in the frozen plains west of the Dnieper. In order to defend huge areas of the western banks of the Dnieper River, German Army Group South and Army Group A put together two panzer and two field armies, from north to south. They were supported by both Hungarian and Romanian forces. In total, there were ninety-three divisions including eighteen panzer and four panzergrenadier divisions, two motorized brigades, three heavy panzer battalions of Tiger tanks, eighteen Sturmgeschütz Assault Gun Brigades, a battalion of 'Elefant' tank destroyers, a mixture of artillery and PaK battalions, including pioneer engineering units. Almost half of the German troops, and three-quarters of the Panzerwaffe that were employed on the Eastern Front were to take part in the defence of the west bank of Ukraine.

A photograph taken in early winter showing a Waffen-SS Sd.Kfz.251 Ausf.D on a road passing winter-clad SS troops. In January 1944, in just one week, Red Army forces had advanced to a depth of nearly 60 miles – completely clearing German forces from the Kyiv and Zhytomyr regions, including a number of districts in and around Vinnitsa and Rovno.

A whitewashed StuG.III can be seen on a dirt track supporting infantry. On 5 January, the Soviet 2nd Ukrainian Front launched what was known as the Kirovograd offensive. One of its first objectives was to stem the III Panzer Corps attacks which were causing considerable problems to the Russian advance in the Kirovograd region. Losses to both German troops and armour were massive.

A StuG.III crew can be seen in the 'Korsun pocket'. Some 50,000 men, comprised of a total of six German divisions, including the elite SS 'Wiking' and the SS 'Sturmbrigade Wallonien'. The 'Wiking' division was the only armoured unit in the pocket with some 43 tanks and assault guns. Two assault gun battalions provided an additional 27 assault guns. With these tanks and assault guns they were ordered to smash out of the pocket.

A StuG.III Ausf.G on the move through a Ukrainian village. During March, Army Group South was forced to make a slow fighting withdrawal to the Dniester River, on the border with Romania.

(**Above**) A stationary whitewashed Pz.Kpfw.IV can be seen on the edge of a burning town.

(**Opposite, above**) A StuG.III passes a knocked-out KV-1 Russian tank during its withdrawal westwards through Ukraine. In order to try and stabilise the deteriorating situation, the II.SS.Panzer-Corps, which consisted of the 9th SS Panzer-Division 'Hohenstaufen' and the 10th SS.Panzer-Division 'Frundsberg', was rushed to the Eastern Front from France.

(**Opposite, below**) A winter-clad panzergrenadier takes cover behind a knocked out Pz.KPfw.IV with hull and turret armoured skirts (*Schürzen*). He is armed with a captured PPSh-41 machine gun.

Tiger tank crews and commanders confer before resuming operations.

A long column of StuG.IIIs roll along a snowy road during operations in the winter of 1944. The battles that raged west of the Dnieper River were regarded as the most important events in 1944. However, both troops and armour were not able to contain proper cohesion on the battlefield.

An interesting photograph showing artillery troops onboard a Sd.Kfz.11 towing the 15cm sIG 33 (Schweres Infanteriegeschütz 33 or heavy infantry gun). This was the standard German heavy infantry gun used throughout the war.

A battery of StuG.III Ausf.G crosses a frozen plain moving to the front. Between 1943 and 1944, the StuG was gradually called upon for offensive and defensive fire support, where it was gradually embroiled in an anti-tank role trying to stem the might of the Red Army.

A crewmember is repairing an Sd.Kfz.250. The vehicle was a basic troop carrier and used widely as an armoured personnel carrier for reconnaissance units and carry scout sections.

A Panther crossing a frozen snowy plain fully laden with winter clad infantry hitching a lift.

A Panther can be seen leaving a village with panzergrenadiers marching the opposite direction.

Snow is being removed from a road for a column of Pz.Kpfw.IVs in order to speed movement for an unidentified regiment.

A soldier loading a 15cm Nebelwerfer 42 projectile weighing some 34kg. These rockets were not very accurate and the Germans relied on blanketing the area with a heavy concentration of fire.

A column of Waffen-SS Sd.Kfz.10 are seen withdrawing from the front.

An Sd.Kfz.2 half-track passes a muddy village. This tracked vehicle with a single front wheel was better known as the Kleines Kettenkraftrad HK 101. The vehicle was commonly seen on the Eastern Front where they were used to lay communication cables, pull heavy loads and carry soldiers through the deep mud.

(**Above**) A VW type 82 'Kubelwagen' has halted along a very muddy road and the driver converses with other soldiers.

(**Opposite, above**) A column of armoured vehicles and animal draught hauling supplies are seen withdrawing to another line of defence. By this period of operations in Ukraine, both troops and armour were irrevocably stretched along a very thin front, with many of them rarely reaching the proper operating level. In front of the advancing Red Army, Panzer divisions were often broken up and split among hastily constructed battle groups or Kampfgruppe drawn from a motley collection of armoured formations.

(**Opposite, below**) On a reconnaissance mission and a scouting unit can be seen with an Sd.Kfz.250.

(**Above**) A Pz.Kpfw.IV can be seen out in field during a defensive action. For the defence of Ukraine, Hitler required every soldier on the front line to make an effective resistance in the face of overwhelming strength.

(**Opposite, above**) The crew of a 15cm Nebelwerfer pose for the camera in front of their Panzerwerfer 42 auf Maultier, Sd.Kfz.4/1. The Panzerwerfer 42 auf Maultier was used for larger scale rocket barrages against Soviet positions where a large bombardment of a large area would be more effective than more accurate artillery fire.

(**Opposite, below**) A column of camouflaged Marder.III Ausf.H make their way along a road bound for the front. For the offensive, the Germans of Army Group North Ukraine comprised of two Panzer armies and the 1st Hungarian Army.

(**Above**) Infantry hitch a lift on board a column of Tigers as it advances along a road. Once the tank had moved up to the front lines, the soldiers would dismount and go into action.

(**Opposite, above**) A crew member can be seen loading ammunition into an Elefant tank destroyer in Ukraine during the summer of 1944. Whilst this was a powerful German tank destroyer, the Red Army had produced a handbook on how to kill these tanks showing weak spots and the distance required for Russian tank crews to successfully penetrate its thick armour. In April, thirty-seven of these vehicles were issued to the 2nd and 3rd companies of Schwere Panzerjäger-Abteilung 653 (sPzJgrAbt 653) and sent by train to the Tarnopol battles in Ukraine.

(**Opposite, below**) A crew member poses in front of an Sd.Kfz.10/5 late modification vehicle equipped with a 2cm FlaK 38.

(**Above**) A well-concealed StuG.III inside a forest. In August, Army Group North Ukraine transferred ten divisions from Army Group South Ukraine in order to try and bolster the front and prevent the Red Army from driving its forces out of Western Ukraine into Poland. These divisions included three Hungarian divisions, six StuG brigades and the 501st Heavy Tank Battalion, equipped with Tiger IIs.

(**Opposite, above**) A column of Tiger tanks wade across a river. During the last weeks of July, a frantic attempt by the Panzerwaffe was made to stem the rout of the Soviet drive into Poland. Army Group North Ukraine tried its best to contain its meagre position on the River Bug, whilst remnants of Army Group Centre tied with all available resources to create a solid front line Kaunas, Bialystok-Brest and assemble what was left of its forces on both its flanks. But between Army Group Centre and Army Group North, German positions were depleted.

(**Below**) A Pz.Kpfw.IV advances across a field followed by an Sd.Kfz.251. By the early summer large areas of troop and armoured concentrations west of the Dnieper were battered to the point of where they were paralysed. Despite the fact that new defensive lines were constructed, troop strength and the lack of weapons and armour were so depleted that nothing could be done to avert many units becoming encircled and then annihilated.

(**Opposite, above**) Luftwaffe Flak crew can be seen with a prime mover hauling an 8.8cm Flak gun.

(**Opposite, below**) Two StuG.IIIs are rolling along a dirt track through a village south of Lwow. On 24 July 1944, the 1st Panzer Army ordered to defend the city of Lwow and its front to the south. However, due to the overwhelming strength of the Red Army, two days later the 1st Panzer begun to withdraw in order to avoid complete decimation. The city fell with relative ease.

(**Above**) An SS Panther crew pose for the camera. With the capture of the city of Lwow, German forces had been completely forced out from Western Ukraine. Now that Ukraine had been liberated Soviet forces could now attack across the Vistula with the objective of capturing the city of Sandomierz, which was in German held southern Poland.

Appendix One

German Army Group South Order of Battle 1941–42

Commanded by Field Marshal Gerd von Rundstedt
Chief of Staff – Lt. Gen. Georg von Sodenstern

German Sixth Army
Field Marshal Walther von Reichenau

XVII Corps (General of Infantry Werner Kienitz)
56th Infantry Division (Lt. Gen. Karl von Oven)
62nd Infantry Division (Lt. Gen. Walter Keiner)
XXIX Corps (General of Infantry Hans von Obstfelder)
44th Infantry Division (Lt. Gen. Friedrich Siebert)
111th Infantry Division (Lt. Gen. Otto Stapf)
299th Infantry Division (Lt. Gen. Willi Moser)
XXXXIV Corps (General of Infantry Friedrich Koch)
9th Infantry Division (Lt. Gen. Siegmund Freiherr von Schleinitz)
297th Infantry Division (Lt. Gen. Max Pfeffer)
LV Corps (General of Infantry Erwin Vierow)
75th Infantry Division (Lt. Gen. Ernst Hammer)
57th Infantry Division (Lt. Gen. Oskar Blümm)
168th Infantry Division (Lt. Gen. Hans Mundt)
298th Infantry Division (Mj. Gen. Walther Graeßner)

Panzergruppe 1
Colonel General Paul Ludwig Ewald von Kleist

III Corps (mot.) (General of Cavalry Eberhard von Mackensen)
13th Panzer Division (Lt. Gen. Friedrich-Wilhelm von Rothkirch und Panthen)
14th Panzer Division (Lt. Gen. Friedrich Kühn)
25th Infantry Division (mot.) (Lt. Gen. Erich-Heinrich Clößner)
XIV Corps (mot.) (General of Infantry Gustav Anton von Wietersheim)
9th Panzer Division (Lt. Gen. Alfred Ritter von Hubicki)
SS-Division (mot.) Leibstandarte SS Adolf Hitler (SS-Obergruppenführer Sepp Dietrich
SS-Wiking Division (SS-Brigadeführer Felix Steiner)

XXXXVIII Corps (mot.) (General of Panzer Werner Kempf)
11th Panzer Division (Lt. Gen. Ludwig Crüwell)
16th Panzer Division (Lt. Gen. Hans-Valentin Hube)
16th Infantry Division (mot.) (Lt. Gen. Sigfrid Henrici)

German 17th Army

General of Infantry Carl-Heinrich von Stülpnagel

IV Corps (General of Infantry Viktor von Schwedler)
24th Infantry Division (Lt. Gen. Hans von Tettau)
71st Infantry Division (Lt. Gen. Alexander von Hartmann)
262nd Infantry Division (Lt. Gen. Edgar Theisen [de])
295th Infantry Division (Lt. Gen. Herbert Geitner)
296th Infantry Division (Lt. Gen. Wilhelm Stemmermann)
XXXXIX Mountain Corps (General of Infantry – Ludwig Kübler)
68th Infantry Division (Lt. Gen. Georg Braun)
257th Infantry Division (Lt. Gen. Karl Sachs)
1st Mountain Division (Lt. Gen. Hubert Lanz)
LII Corps (General of Infantry Kurt von Briesen)
101st Light Infantry Division (Lt. Gen. Erich Marcks)
97th Light Infantry Division (Mj. Gen. Maximilian Fretter-Pico)
100th Light Infantry Division (Mj. Gen. Werner Sanne)
Hungarian Fast Corps (Gen. Béla Miklós)
1st Hungarian Motorized Brigade (Bg. Gen. Jeno Major)
2nd Hungarian Motorized Brigade (Bg. Gen. János Vörös)
1st Hungarian Cavalry Brigade (Bg. Gen Antal Vattay [hu])
Slovak Expeditionary Army Group (Gen. Ferdinand Čatloš)
Slovakian Mobile Brigade (LTC. Rudolf Pilfousek [pl])
1st Slovakian Infantry Division (Lt. Gen. Antonin Pulanich)
2nd Slovakian Infantry Division (Lt. Gen. Alexander Čunderlík [sk])

Romanian Army Group Antonescu

General Ion Antonescu

Romanian Third Army (Lt. Gen. Petre Dumitrescu)
Romanian 4th Army Corps (Mj. Gen. Constantin Sănătescu)
6th Infantry Division (Br. Gen. Romulus Ioanovici [ro])
7th Infantry Division (Br. Gen. Olimpiu Stavrat [ro])
Cavalry Corps (Mj. Gen. Ioan Mihail Racoviță
5th Cavalry Brigade (Col. Vasile Măinescu [ro])
8th Cavalry Brigade (Col. Ioan Dănescu [ro])
Mountain Corps (Mj. Gen. Gheorghe Avramescu)
1st Mountain Brigade (Br. Gen. Mihail Lascăr)
2nd Mountain Brigade (Br. Gen. Ioan Dumitrache)
4th Mountain Brigade (Br. Gen. Gheorghe Manoliu)
Romanian Fourth Army (Lt. Gen. Nicolae Ciupercă
Romanian 3rd Army Corps (Mj. Gen. Vasile Atanasiu)

Guards Division (Mj. Gen. Nicolae Sova [ro])
15th Infantry Division (Mj. Gen. Cosma Marin Popescu [ro])
35th Reserve Divisions (Br. Gen. Emil Procopiescu [ro])
Romanian 5th Army Corps (Lt. Gen. Gheorghe Leventi [ro])
Border Division (Br. Gen. Gheorghe Potopeanu [ro])
21st Division (Mj. Gen. Cristache Popescu [ro])
Romanian 11th Army Corps (Mj. Gen. I. Aurelian)
two fortress brigades

Other assets:
Romanian 2nd Army Corps (Mj. Gen. Nicolae Macici)
9th Infantry Division (Br. Gen. Hugo Schwab)
10th Infantry Division (Br. Gen. Ion Glogojanu)
7th Cavalry Brigade (Col. Gheorghe Săvoiu [ro])
11th Infantry Division (Br. Gen. David Popescu)

German 11th Army

Colonel General Eugen Ritter von Schobert

XI Corps (General of Infantry Joachim von Kortzfleisch)
76th Infantry Division (Lt. Gen. Maximilian de Angelis)
239th Infantry Division (Lt. Gen. Ferdinand Neuling)
1st Romanian Armoured Division (Bg. Gen. Ioan Sion)
6th Romanian Cavalry Brigade (Mg. Gen. Aurel Racovitză [ro])

XXX Corps (General of Infantry Hans von Salmuth)
198th Infantry Division (Lt. Gen. Otto Röttig)
8th Romanian Infantry Division (Bg. Gen. Alexandru Orăsanu [ro])
13th Romanian Infantry Division (Bg. Gen. Gheorghe Rozin [ro])
14th Romanian Infantry Division (Bg. Gen. Gheorghe Stavrescu [ro])

LIV Corps (General of Cavalry Erick-Oskar Hansen)
50th Infantry Division (Lt. Gen. Karl-Adolf Hollidt)
170th Infantry Division (Lt. Gen. Walter Wittke [de])
5th Romanian Infantry Division (Bg. Gen. Petre Vlădescu)

Italian Expeditionary Corps (Lt. Gen. Giovanni Messe)
9th Infantry Division 'Pasubio' (Gen. Vittorio Giovanelli)
52nd Infantry Division 'Torino' (Gen. Luigi Manzi)
3rd Cavalry Division 'Principe Amedeo Duca d'Aosta' (Gen. Mario Marazzani)
22nd Infantry Division (Lt. Gen. Hans Graf von Sponeck)

Appendix Two

German Army Group South Order of Battle 1943–44

Army Group South, 1943

Commander – Field Marshal Erich von Manstein

4th Panzer Army
1st Panzer Army
8th Army
6th Army
Luftflotte 2
Luftflotte 4

Army Group A

Commander – General Ewald von Kleist

17th Army
6th Army
Romanian Cavalry Division

Army Group Centre

Commander – General Gunther von Kluge

2nd Army

(Army Group Centre's part in the Dnieper battle was brief and operations halted on October 3, 1943)

Army Group A, 1944

Commander – General Ferdinand Schörner

17th Army
Romanian Mountain Corps
1st Mountain Division
2nd Mountain Division

Appendix Three

German Army Group North Ukraine Order of Battle 1944

Commander: General Josef Harpe

18th Artillery Division
4th Panzer Army
XLVI Panzer Corps
- 16th Panzer Division
- 17th Panzer Division
- 291st Infantry Division
- 340th Infantry Division

XXXXII Army Corps
- 72nd Infantry Division
- 88th Infantry Division

LVI Panzer Corps
- 26th Infantry Division
- 342nd Infantry Division
- 1st Ski Jäger Division

VIII Corps
- 5th Jäger Division
- 211th Infantry Division
- 12th Hungarian Reserve Division
- 1st Panzer Army

XIII Army Corps
- 361st Infantry Division
- 454th Security Division
- 14th Waffen Grenadier Division of the SS (1st Ukrainian)

XXXXVIII Panzer Corps
- 96th Infantry Division
- 349th Infantry Division
- 359th Infantry Division

III Panzer Corps
- 1st Panzer Division
- 8th Panzer Division

XXIV Panzer Corps
- 20th Panzergrenadier Division
- 100th Jäger Division
- 75th Infantry Division
- 254th Infantry Division
- 371st Infantry Division

LIX Army Corps
- 1st Infantry Division
- 208th Infantry Division
- 20th Hungarian Infantry Division
- 1st Hungarian Army

XI Army Corps
- 101st Jäger Division
- 24th Hungarian Infantry Division
- 25th Hungarian Infantry Division
- 18th Hungarian Reserve Division

VIIth Hungarian Army Corps
- 16th Hungarian Infantry Division
- 68th Infantry Division
- 168th Infantry Division

VIth Hungarian Army Corps
- 27th Hungarian Light Division
- 1st Hungarian Mountain Brigade
- Hungarian First Army Reserve
- 2nd Hungarian Panzer Division
- 2nd Hungarian Mountain Brigade
- 19th Hungarian Reserve Division
- Luftflotte 4
- VIII. Fliegerkorps
- Luftflotte 6

Notes